Cristina Pérez Díaz

From the Founding of the Country

Winter Editions, 2025

*From the Founding
of the Country*

Para mi país

Cada isla nos seduce, nos obliga a naufragar,
a llegar, llegar, llegar, a inventar un verbo nuevo.

Manuel Ramos Otero

O I say these are not the parts and poems of the body
    only, but of the soul,
O I say now these are the soul!

Walt Whitman

The Garden of Limbs

1.

Limbs of each other.
Limbs to be remembered by no one.
We alone.
We grew a garden.
Every dead Sunday we grew a garden of limbs.
Every dead Sunday a garden of daggers in our thighs.
Not to be remembered
That every Sunday we neglected this labor
Of founding a country.
And stayed in bed.
Each growing limbs inside the other.
And not only on Sundays.
All week long, for years.
We neglected the task repeatedly.
Even now, to be honest,
We are really just lying in bed.

2.

But the grass will forgive us.
And the sun will forgive us.
And the cow and the horse and the seagull.
And the sea more than anything will forgive us.
In fact, they'll be pleased.
And the multiple islands at which we didn't arrive,
They too will forgive us.

3.

Today—dust, I myself become dust.
I do not ask, I become
Dust in love with your dust.
Yesterday I was walking carrying all the wounds.
I myself the wounded woman.
Two eyes in front of two solitary eyes.
Milk flowing from the wounds.
Dust. Today we shatter like dust, one body
Against the other, milk and dust
Form roses of mud.

4.

I swallow the mud and the milk and the roses.
I swallow all of this.
I love it.
All the milk rushing.
I become all the mud and the milk and the roses.
And we can enter the flesh,
Finally, without making repairs.

5.

Massacred—it was beautiful early summer.

6.

But now it's all forgotten.
Dust.
Again, we bury the city in the past.
Again, we rub our bodies against each other.
Again, less and less is left of us.

Maybe the skin of the roses is left.
Maybe the whizz of limbs, heads, stone, wood, iron.
Maybe our limbs.
Maybe your body is left.

Your body I will found onto the landscape.
And on the landscape a home.
And I will cut your outline and fold it.
And the paper in the shape of a boat.
I will sail you.

I promise endless expeditions.

7.

To what islands? On what boat?
If no one is waiting for us on any shore?
But we row by the light of the moon and win
Every single battle, to enter
The flesh finally, without making repairs.
Today—dust.

8.

We will see:
Our country will not be a country of memories.
But memories must be founded.
We will see:
Even when everything must pass, only this much
Let me hold:
We are founding a country on the pale green grass.

9.

But we stand here and we look
At the layer of mauve that covers our city at dusk.
We contemplate it simply and we love it.
And then we go back to bed and to our bodies.
And we see that there is also a layer of dusk.
We need a new verb, what would it be, elegy?

10.

And I open the window for us to gaze at the vast
    landscape of our country:
Look now, a swift line of horses.

And with paper and pencil, I'll draw for you as many
    flowers.

And I'll ask you, woman:
Where is the middle point between my body and a
    million universes?

You will meet me there.

11.

I celebrate it and celebrate myself—dust.
And here we are standing on this spot with our souls.
On this spot I stand.
Sideways, curious to see what we will found next.
On what shore will your body dwell.
In what cave will you ease for me the darkness.

I see clearly now I've sweated through fogs.
In search of your eyes—grass.
Of your pale-green kisses—dust.
Of your grassy lips.
The shore of your breath.

And you have breasts!
Milky breasts!
I really like it when they are erect.

I am erect!
I am myself a jutting rock!
Where I am standing now!
From where now I turn my gaze away!
To the vast landscape!
Our country!
Our own country!
Dust!

12.

But we will call it fire, that reverberation of the loved
    one inside.
And that is how we will discover duration.
In analogy with the smoldering feeling.
And we will discover the end of duration
Of which physical death is no evidence.

But the end of love, everyone knows that
Is the true mark of finitude.

13.

Later, later I stop.
In the future I stop.
Next Tuesday, maybe
Next Tuesday I'll stop.

But now is the bird there
Near the wild flowers.
It is now there.
Now there.
Now there.
It brings the meadow to itself.

Myself there,
Myself,
There is that in me,
There is my self.

Two bodies wrenched under the sun.

14.

We begin.
Our country is plenty of us at 27.
Let us meet there: in between our ages.
This is the poem and this is the time.
We begin now.

I bequeath myself to the dust to grow from the grass I
 love.
Here we start.
On the rocky shore.

Only the lull of the shore I like.
Only the lull.

Tenderly I curl up on the grass.
Spreading my green heart
To gather us in bed
Under the faint red roofs of our mouths.

Only reality I like.
Only dust.

15.

Night plunges its tongue into the brook.
Right there, where the brook puts out of the roots of the
 old tree.
And flows to the meadow. There. There is my script.

It sails me.

16.

And now the night sees that it has nighted.
And what is night but that body on the streets
Of desire, but your dark sweat turning my flesh to a
    sponge.
But the mouth, forgetful of the past.
Your bush blooming in my tongue, how noble.
The feebleness of the rose, how
It turns itself into itself into itself.
To die of too much night in the verb dust.

How black is the sea.

How every island is an invitation.
To wreck or to arrive.

We need a new verb, what would it be—limb?

17.

But we will acknowledge the new lands!
We will salute every city!
We will report on heroism!

We will sing the song of companionship!
We will found our own ideal of womanly love!
Indicating it in us!

Who, but us, should be the poet of comrades?!
We will lift the smoldering fires!
We need a new verb, what would it be?

Sunday Expeditions

Catalogue of Ships

Cat was sick
She said so she could miss my reading last night.
Today, morning, I replied, here's a recipe:
Two liters of water
One Emergen-C every four hours
Go to Yoga
Rest
Use a Neti Pot
What's a Neti Pot, she asked
I said omg it will change your life
It's a nose irrigator, thinking she is a rather delicate flower
I didn't write *that* and the messaging came to an end
Even though I went as far as to suggest singing

I wanted to go on and get into the thick of it
I expected, after the banalities of the situation
Of our bodies today, a little ill, something would glow in
    the words
Like Cat would ask how did it go, the reading
And I'd tell her how exciting, a nightingale
Fluttered over my chest all night long
But as she didn't respond to this sign, I too was silenced

Then I went out to the street, to Macy's, to buy our
    wedding rings
Gonzalo and I got married last year
We were anxious about his status once Trump was in power
We didn't get the rings back then, but now we're having
    the interview
And it's gotta *look* real

Sitting down as the copy of our past couple, dinner last
    night was by far better
than the original
We ordered:
Five fried pork dumplings
One spicy ramen
One ramen, non-spicy
One Sapporo
One Soju
The waiter wrongly assumed the spicy was for the man.
We were too full for dessert,
But expanding the time of our encounter, I said I need to
    write a poem about stuff,
a catalogue, tonight,
and as we named the objects on our table, pondering what
    to put on the list,
he laughed.
Whether it was the words or his green eyes,
something glowed.

I took the train back uptown, to my studio, and meditated
    on this garden:
Ramos Otero's roses;
Eliot's lilacs and hyacinths;
Funny, I didn't notice there were briers in Whitman!
And delaying on grass and the perfumes
I continued writing our Constitution, a little under the
    influence of it all:

"Our memories will grow in a garden,
Lulled by the presence of briers and lilacs,
Of hyacinths and grass.
Every morning we are to inscribe them
On the sand, right by the fountain of fresh waters.

We ought to memorialize those islands,
The destroyed ones,
As if surveying from a high tower
The camp where the troops prepare for battle,
Or as if we were counting the fleets,
We will take notice of each and every island, and write it down
For posterity to know, at least. Or,
Most likely,
Moved by desire that so often billows in our inside,
We will neglect the task even of memory.
And we will focus on getting right our smallest details,
Not feeling up to the task of gardening,
We will look at the roses,
As they continue to bloom in our limbs."

And now it's okay to inhabit these lonely regions.
I move my chair a few inches to the right
To use a different corner of the small desk,
Moved by necessity to write this epitaph:

"Muchos murieron en ese puerto,
Y no podemos honrarlos. Ni las listas.
Sería mentira decir que nuestros cuerpos,
Eléctricos, se expanden, para ser, en vida,
Su gran cementerio."

I place this epitaph somewhere with intent:
On the door of the fridge?
As my iPhone's screen saver?
A tattoo on my right arm?

And with this feeling of loss
I return to my body and to this poem.
And as I think about our country, I go back

To the image of a woman I love
And I regain my perspective,
Focusing on the details, our two bodies,
So often they turn our gaze away
From the outside, indoors, microscopic:
Your hands, Josephine,
Your fingers, Josephine,
Your arms, Josephine,
Your shoulders,
Your lips, Josephine,
Your kisses, Josephine,
Your eyes, Josephine,
Your hair,
Your sweat,
Josephine, for my flesh-glass,
Josephine, a folk tune about boats
Dangling in the dockyard, my gray hair,
Josephine,
And my kisses and my lips,
And my shoulders and my arms,
And my fingers and my hands,
Sweated, Josephine,
Poem and body sweated.

Sunday Song

There are no verbs on Sundays
But things do happen

Melting, for instance
Slow or fast, it all depends on the season

When it is not Sunday I eat
Other things and ice cream too

The week happens so fast
There is no time for melting

No licking just swallowing
No bench in the park

But a shivering, transitive sidewalk
Even if the flavor is of bright pink strawberry

The color is not even bitter it's imprecise
It is precisely the lack of precision that bothers me

On Sundays, I take the matter of justice in my hands
I
Cut the day, sharp, with neat borders

I
Draw, strict lines, with my black, fine, point

Everywhere
There is
A surface

Where one
Can intervene

One can fold the edges of anything into something
Else, prettier and softer in its definition
Kind, slow, sweet

And the total sum of the many-folded object
Is an ongoing aria

—For which the word in Greek is the synonym of law
but there are no laws on Sundays—
I sing, only
I sing

To sing is not a verb but an adjective of voice
Or it is movement contained in a noun:

Breath?

I like only reality and so I only like
This day of preparations

Preparation takes time to enter onto time
It remains aloof from motion and sequences and goodbyes

On Sundays I know just to say a fair "Hi"
With strange punctuation, rather vertical and not final

**The Sunday Before the First Expedition,
I Spot Josephine**

And I notice a loud example of laughter
It comes out of the expanded lungs of a tall, corpulent man
He is standing on the sidewalk opposite me
Not laughing

I notice in me the arrival of envy

It rises

Like it rose

Like the roses

Full of red

And then—it's only natural as I go upstairs—I notice the
 two rings:

They are still here

Untouched Unmoved Unrequited

And they bring myself back to myself
And they bring my body back to the situation of my body
A little ill
And they bring my soul to the grassy meadow of my soul
As it is, unaccompanied by birds

This mute moment of realization:
The wedding rings here

Their tiny black boxes

        And the voice on the margins comments:
        "This could have been our paradise"

I take note in my heart of the song
That spontaneously bursts into my computer
It's always *that* song, ha,
I always sing it when it comes to that,
To singing, to one part of myself, to History

        And the voice on the margins comments:
        "This past is now here"

And though I look at the rings,
It is impossible for me to see
The rings.
I see they're circular and golden and, I assume,
Beautiful, as I abstract myself from the rings,
But when I come back to the rings
I see my husband
And I see myself
Two circles
Entrapped in the movement
Of migrations
And nimble citizenships

And I move on to a new task
To organize the whole
Again
To break free from the circle
Which is all I can do, after all
I put order in a different sequence

And then I spot Josephine in the crowd, so naturally!

She is running to me—running!
At the park on this nice evening at the very beginning of fall
It is perfect
I should not forget this moment
I should never forget
This light
This temperature
This color
This breeze
How it is all grounded in itself, tightly
Finished by the delicate brush of Josephine
Running!

When she stops to say Hi!
To *me*.
To *me*!
Sitting down on the bench like no athlete
I accidentally drop all my instruments on the ground
So crisp is the whole

She says sorry like it was her fault
It's the moment, I thought, it's the moments' crispy fault!
How it all falls
Grounded

> And the voice on the margins comments:
> "The mute undivided present"

And the moment suddenly closes onto itself and it's over
There's nothing left
The unknown quantity of my feelings runs away with her

Away, away, away, away
Down the tree-lined pathway
With its withering leaves
Riding the soft-yellow back of the sinking sun

Sunday News

And there will be time for sleeping
To rest our exhausted bodies
And receive the visitations
That come only at night in deep shadows
With low voices, glimmering
They muster and mutter and babble
And we'll stop gnashing our teeth
Surrounded by much water
—This battle to wake up will be over

There will be time for sleeping
It is not possible to remain awake
How am I supposed to take it all in
—How much breath can I offer—
Give me a wide margin to pass out
And comment in passing on the margins of newspapers' leafs
How—I am deeply embarrassed—am I supposed to read
Them So many So often So crowded I edit
I trace with red ink a better version
Let me sleep!

I'll take sunset to bed
For coming back from dreams, we encounter objects
In strange places, just as Archilochus
Back then
Left his shield lying next to a bush
And said later I'll find another one
I now take
Hold of something that is not in the Greek
Only in English can the word *bush* shield me
With that part of your body

But this thickness of air, these overcrowded spaces
A pace so inwrought, packed, chopped, and time does not
Become longer, no, it stays thin, thinner as I too
Wither and decay, and can't
Take it all in. I
Measure myself with an obsession
More similar to the act of diving

But you and I, we will find time for sleeping
Camping on the far edges of our land
We'll claim our sovereign right to slumber

The Future of Dust

But now let's get real
and move to prose.
She,
for there could be no doubt of her sex,
though the fashion of the time did something to disguise it,
she
approaches the founding of a country.

Arms, to be precise, will be used.
Our limbs will be used.

For she meant it in all earnest:
We are founding a country.

She writes off violence and malicious slavery.
She puts them down on the page.

And walks past its borders
leaving the business to the powers of decay

to the rotting materials paper is made of,
hoping that just as matter

becomes invisible to our eyes
violence
and slavery
too
will
come
to
dust.

Perhaps she presumes all too quickly that the spheres that here concern her—the erotic and sentimental—are free from the dangers of the epic dynamics by which men have made history. Should I ask her to take a detour into theory? Or should I presume an informed reader? Please, allow me to send you to the necessary books and to continue my task here, for it is different. This poem tells of two women and of two women alone: Josephine and I. It is a particular task, not engaged at all with universals. They will, they will have to deal with their disagreeables as they sit down at the table to reach a social contract. Yet, the advantage of dealing with particularity is that I can always draw on more particulars and continuously escape the oppressive realm of abstraction our author is so fond of. When all this founding of the country starts to resemble the language of bureaucrats, they can always run to bed. But to continue, I said, let's get real and deal with what they dislike most: blood.

[I insert my own translation of Livy!]

[Let the page bleed!]

Let us settle ourselves, and work and wedge our feet downward through the mud and slush of opinion, and prejudice, and tradition, and delusion, and appearance, that alluvion which covers the globe, through Paris and London, through New York and Boston and Concord, through church and state, through poetry and philosophy and religion, till we come to a hard bottom and rocks in place ... a place where you might found a wall or a state (Thoreau, *Walden*. Ch. II, paragraph 23).

We looked We said We needed
Needed to find Needed to say Needed to settle
How we founded

How we innovated!
How we cheered up!
How we exhausted!

Needed to clash And shine And outstand
Clashed and shone

Will erase!

She said we need a new verb She said it and she found it
It took time and experience The passage of hours Months
Maybe years without writing Yet listening every morning
to the news Immersed in prose She has been using the
dictionary exhaustively Elusive meaning frequently
reminding her This is not your language There's beauty
in dictionaries She reckons Elation even In the swift pace
of the passage from one word to another And the risk of
never coming to an end And I am keeping it to myself
How much time has elapsed between the previous page
and this one What the two lovers have done How they've
felt Whom else they have loved What they have read How
they've been sleeping And the contents of their dreams
The unexpected changes in their skins and shapes of their
bodies The exercises they've practiced And how often the
perception of the passing of the seasons And the mood
swings attached Have made them look at the sunset And
go places Board cars Trains Planes Horses or the changes
In the landscapes outside their windows And why I said
that in the plural Plants have grown in their home And
plants have died in that same home To where they've
also brought groceries And the content of the bags and
whether they were plastic Or paper Or tote bags And the
food they've cooked somehow matters And what kind of
light entered the kitchen At what hour in the spring And
how often they've cleaned the house And the toilet or how
their digestion Has been working as a matter of fact And
what kind of showers And baths They enjoyed together or
individually And if the difference is semantically charged
Or if one of them has failed and then passed An exam and
why are there exams in this country where they themselves
have made the laws of song, and how many times each one

of us has looked at herself in the mirror and fixed, ever so delicately A lock of hair that was flying And whether my hair has grown and I lost count Of how many times they've clipped their nails Out I leave as well the money spent and how it was earned in the first place And every single item they have purchased And the packages they have discarded into the trash bin And walked away Without even a comma Or raising the sort of obvious question such an occasion should be bound to raise For this is in fact our country Or if love withered and died Or was it Josephine who died and I am still calling the lover Josephine For the sake of narrative coherence Or was it because she wanted it that way And it is still an act of love Still moving the poem and the landscape forward As the powerful engine by which one page bleeds into the next But with time they found the verb they'd been looking for Just as they were reading some haphazard document That did not happen to make it into this record

It's good that she has taken to reading theory and history. Not that history repeats itself just because someone does not know it, but founding a country is not something one does by stepping into a boat and reaching a territory and erasing the bad verses. Rhyme demands so much more! Consequences ought to be anticipated! Forms should be studied! Ideals molded! Justice embraced!

What kind of country do the lovers want to erect? What to do with the land and with oneself? Questions begin to pop up like wildflowers. But of one thing she is sure: We are making history. Yet what will our sources be and how are we to gather them? I mean, our bodies. For she takes our bodies to be their primary sources. Masses of limbs, full of cheap moisturizers and sun block, dipped in drugs from within, wrinkled, continuously decaying and even secretly rotting, the cells trying ever so hard to keep them alive, and it all keeps falling apart, the germs sucking out the oh so precious elasticity of their skins and the glow that's left, and bacteria, viruses, at times they are swollen, inflamed, sore, bloated, burnt, dried out, scratched, scorched.

Brief:

Less and less and less and less is left of us

What narrative are we to create and keep for posterity
—with what energy—
once we've spent all there is, only to keep
and to keep together our microscopic
mess? For how could they ever narrate
their limbs keeping it faithful to the reality
of their limbs? The narrative keeps conglomerating
the bodies
iat the same time it
tears them apart! Oh,
but with that smile she's a keeper.

They will look back at themselves
and, from a distance,
they'll seem
complete,
composed,
even heroic,
perfectly tight
and even
bronzed and even
beautiful.

Will that be enough?

Or should we take this more seriously and look for models in the recesses of libraries and archives and in the silences of the material record?

—For how can it ever be helpful for our country that I
translate some old man's history as if it were a paradigm
and insert him into the pages of our Constitution as a
catastrophic editorial practice?
—Well... to entrap... frame him within our narrative.
—But no, to us he'll be no example. From the pages of
this poem
from which at some point we ourselves shall be erased,
I'll weave for you a chariot
to make our glorious entrance into our country,
and as we ride, the sides of the roads will be crowded
with people shouting, welcoming—wooo
waaa ehhh wohaaa woohooo, they'll shout
at us, their enthusiasm, at us, the founders
of this country, and we'll greet them warmly
in return, not knowing what else to do in this sudden
position and, renouncing
the task of spectacle,
we'll ask them to go home and sleep tenderly
and tend to the grass and the roses,
to the papaya tree!
and the bright lemon!
to the ground full of pineapples!
to the panapén going wild!
to the avocados!
to the sour cherry!
and the forgotten zapote!
also the mamey!
to the quenepas!
to the sour oranges!
and stepping down from our dream,
Josephine!,

we will get to work!
with everyone else!
to purify the waters!

Thus far she has been avoiding the issue of money and how they're going to deal with the market economy. But didn't Marx himself say it, language is sensuous? And it was also he who added a thing transcends (loses, sheds [sic]) its sensuousness when it becomes a commodity. It's only an easy inference that language, being a thing, also sheds its sensual quality when it becomes a commodity. Yet she'd rather talk about something else, for she doesn't understand a thing about money. Better to improve citational practices, better to insert a passage from Rosa Luxemburg that says at such moments I think of you and I would like so much to pass on this magical key to you, so that always and in all situations you would live in a joyful euphoria, and it is swiftly decided they will live off the fruits of their labor.

Beat me, beat me, beat me!

(she screams euphorically out of the window
to the tall mountains
to the dark oaks
to the willow-trees
and they echo
and beat her
in return
absent
though they are
from this tropical landscape)

Such is the sound and the impetus of love!

But she is taken aback. Why did I write this poem instead of hitting on Josephine? What megalomaniac decides to found a country because she has fallen in love? And what does love, of all things, have to do with the business of founding a country? If only she were able to yell, with lungs immense: *To drive free! To love free! To dash reckless and dangerous!*—that's one thing she's never been: dangerous. But we are past the point of no return and she continues writing in ecstasy:

with each scream more embarrassed at the pretension of honesty that thus far has been ruling her actions and the construction of her persona. How undignified of me. I've been earnest but now she is founding a country and she needs to get things really clear. Her verbs for instance and how they're going to dictate the rhythm of her breath or how the landscape will carry them places, lifting trails of dust as they ride yellow horses.

Parenthesis

The lover stands still in front of a thousand universes: decomposition, waiting, expectation, contemplating the landscape, lying on the bed, reverberating. But the lovers embark on countless expeditions, always in their quest of founding a country. It's crisp and clear that the sea and the land and the vastness are of paper, and that paper and ink they shall remain. But there is a quest that is real, that of finding a new verb. Or, as it is more likely, I'll find that the right verb is missing and trace, at least, with your delicate fingers, the outlines of the hole.

To Sail!

1.

we begin with two countries
two pairs of flickering wings
two countries

we begin with two ships
metaphors of countries
two possibilities of wreckage
at least, two expectant harbors

we begin with two lovers
metaphors for the boats
two songs tramping the desert of the night
two bodies wounded on the shore

2.

stretched and still lies midnight
it rains on the ceiling of the phantom house i remember
look
two great hulls on the breast of darkness

your shadow multiplies in the flickering water
our vessel sinks slowly
into the spiral stairs to those forests
where we want to get lost

3.

yet time remains irretrievable
we could turn to the topic of children
we are two women and soon there'll be more
let them decide how they want to deal with the issue

but ask the island if she wants to receive our offspring
go to the rocky coasts and plead
our cases, that we are giving birth
to the next gods

you and i
let us ground this moment on our flesh
and let time close onto itself
so neat, and even tender
like the sun when it rises over a high mountain
only the size of a quail's egg

4.

and at some point now we will have to deal with grief
that comes from massacres and every sort of death

5.

but push my life off the cliff of your bed-boat
like a bridegroom that never belonged to the edge
and turn my flesh into those dreams where it still smells
    of dreams
you, tighten the night to my thighs
and my lips
and your bones made of ashes
your anxious suntan
your blood
all dismembered in this lightless basement
some neighbors upstairs like to call soul,
but melt for me the falling blocks of our city in ruins
till it doesn't taste like dust
like it got dusted and beaten
by our comings and goings, dawn and dusk
you, there, suicide me to pleasure

6.

let us depart now
this is the poem and this is the time!

there's a country awaiting, we are bound
this is the poem and this is the time!

vast landscapes, plenty of our bodies
this is the poem and this is the time!

tenderly, i'll weave for you the curling grass
this is the poem and this is the time!

tenderly, tenderly i'll take care of the phantoms
this is the poem and this is the time!

tenderly, tenderly, tenderly, i'll take care of the briers
this is the poem and this is the time!

the fleet is ready, our limbs unscathed
this is the poem and this is the time!

our verbs are depleted, the sea is rising
this is the poem and this is the time!

7.

when i think about
the landscapes
of our country
i think not of the desert
i see the roses
and behind the roses
grass
an expanse of green
a line of horses
in the background
a tall ridge of mountains
not with snow
i see
your body
and i see the sea
that has no thorns
that doesn't leave us
bare and naked
in the cold
but warmth
washes our skin
this landscape i see under the midday sun

(there are voices
we won't be alone)

the sand will call in other bodies to rest
(i see their limbs
how they move carelessly
all flesh and no reins
under crisp bright pink bathing suits)
our fellow companions

Canto primero

La primera mañana

—Llego a esta costa neblinosa,
traigo en los ojos nuestros cuerpos enturbiados,
el paisaje está, preciso,
detrás de su propia imagen,
pero no,
no es el sabor de tus fluidos sudorosos en mis labios
lo que nubla y difumina los bordes de lo visto,
por más que impregnes el aire con tus sales,
es el paisaje.

—Es el paisaje que se dibuja y desdibuja de frente,
tan arraigado en sí, tan fundado, el paisaje
va burlando las formas que le di cuando lo esperábamos,
tan precisas.

—Aquí toda la tierra está por trabajarse, pero crecen
por sí mismos tantos frutos, junto a algo
como parques, como casas, como sitios
donde una vez alguien aseguró, con las ligeras amarras de
    las cosas,
la vida en anaqueles plenos–digo, por robarle economía
    al lenguaje
y no tener que entrar en listas minuciosas de materias
que de todas formas se perdieron—

—crecen, crecen verdes, altas, por sí mismas, sin orgullo,
sin saberse pan y único futuro, las flores
—no son jacintos, no son lilas,
ni siquiera rosas, bien miradas, tienen pétalos distintos,
no se enroscan en sí mismas y no sé—tomo una pausa
para dudar—

si es verdad que quieren multiplicarse en nuestros
    muslos—

—Aquí siempre es domingo,
aquí hay abundancia de fosas,
donde podría sembrarse,
pero no,
esto no es un cementerio junto al mar,
tampoco hay que creer que son jardines,

—estamos vivas de milagro, después de haber corrido
en línea horizontal sobre el paisaje
atestado de bombas y aún así,
aquí crecen por sí mismas tantas flores
—no son rosas, te digo, no lo son,
puede que sean peces cansados del agua
sucia y no sabemos, atolondradas, relentecidas,
tan sumidas en la niebla de nuestros mutuos párpados,
cómo leer, cómo cantar digo,
el trino cacofónico de estas aves de la mañana—

Nada nuestros cuerpos

—Pero nosotras somos nada.

—Llegamos y pisar la tierra nos ennada.

—No es que hayamos llegado y todo es polvo,

—pero sí que al pisar apenas se levantan polvaredas, mira:

—hemos perdido el peso de los pies a la llegada

—como si la primera pisada estuviera siendo en verdad

—primera, anterior incluso al polvo.

—El paisaje nos dará las nuevas formas: no es salvaje,

—como lo que dicen que hubo antes, antes, en ese antes

—imaginado y previo a la llegada

—que no se puede leer. No.

—Es lo después,

—no de nosotras, de nosotras no, después de todo, lo anterior,

—incluso al polvo,

—y aún así es por sí mismo, no es salvaje, lo salvaje

—presupone una mente que lo nombre así,

—pero aquí es todo tan nuevo

—como para presuponer nada,

—es lo que está y lo que llega, nosotras mismas, mira

—cómo vamos surgiendo en nuestros pasos.

—No hay caballos.

—No hay horizontes.

—Los animales nos rodean, lo sabemos,

—por el murmullo con que invaden la atmósfera

—y no es el mar,

—o no tan solo,

—lo que ruge acompasando este caminar incierto.

—No hay amenazas.

—No se nos paran los pelos,

—domesticados quedan por la humedad del aire,

—suavecitos, como durmiendo en nuestras pieles nectarinas.

—Tenemos veintisiete años, no lo olvides.

Las habitaciones del placer

pero es una cosa de esquinas redondeadas, de pisos pulidos, o más bien gastados, depende de cómo se comprenda lo que brilla, por la frecuencia de los mismos pasos sobre la misma precisa, superficie, es volverse masas circulares sudorosas de flores, mucho más hechas para ese tipo de tacto que a la vez huele, hay que enceguecer un poco y tantear con gusto dactilar los pliegues delicadísimos de cada cuerpo en la mañana, recién venidos de las otras regiones en las que no sabemos, hay que verificar, durante el día, cada tanto, que algún doblez no se nos haya vuelto agudo, ir pasando con la piedra caliza sobre los callos para que cada cosa carezca de filos, en una casa, alguna, las hay de todo tipo, si sabemos bien cómo duelen las habitaciones cuando se vacían, que nos duele el espacio como si fuera un órgano perdido, y puede que lo sea pues también respira, que a la casa traemos plantas y animales para que sea santuario y espejo de las sensaciones, para que subrayen la fragilidad que tan fácil olvidamos en nosotras mismas, no, no es nunca un edificio, el jardín de nuestros miembros multiplicados en las superficies, en los tiestos, en las jarras de agua dulce, es siempre verde, con sensación de lluvia ligera tras los muros, adentro sólo un poco de rocío y unas voces que hacen eco de los pájaros afuera, sólo lo domesticado, sólo lo domesticado, así como va tendiendo lazos con la lengua, con los ojos, con las manos,
con los hombros,
el pelo gris,
los brazos,
los labios,
los dedos,
el sudor,

Los nuevos edificios / Islas flotantes

1

Aprendemos a vivir con animales,
en nuestras habitaciones ellos buscan
la memoria escondida de un paisaje
menos trabajado, por ello también
menos apto para el juego.

2

Aprendemos a jugar, en estos espacios
que son suaves
a pesar de que, tras la ventana,
parpadea el aviso de catástrofe.

3

Es necesario el tacto de sus pieles, sus abrigos inocentes,
su mirada que no sabe del futuro y no sospecha
que en estas manos benévolas
se ha consumido tanto resquicio de mundo.

4

Desde esos ojos cada cosa adquiere una forma inhumana:
un libro es una cama, un tiesto es una choza
donde tomar las horas en el fresco de la noche,
el cuarto de visitas, cerrado por días abre
otra dimensión, como partir de cero.

5

Vamos construyendo edificios nuevos
—de los viejos tantos quedaron sin oficio,
afeando el paisaje con sus muros inútiles,
ocupando espacio a la maleza
que ya por fin ha clamado de nuevo su ciudad—

6

en ellos ahora venimos a jugar y son distintos.

7

Para empezar, respiran; en vez de paredes
con diseños de flores, hay flores
y hay árboles con frutos.
Aquí se vive y aunque sí, se duerme,
no venimos a descansar los miembros
tras largas jornadas laborales.
Aquí pasamos los días, incluso los soleados,

8

al interior de los jardines, donde el sol
siempre es clemente y la lluvia cae en forma de cortinas,
recordatorio lúcido que siempre hay un afuera,

9

pero aquí sin amenaza, los animales y nosotras,
estamos listas para las inundaciones.

Author's Note

I wanted to translate Manuel Ramos Otero's *Invitación al polvo* into English, so I started playing around. It's not an easy one to translate and English is not my first language. I looked for companions in the game. It might have happened fortuitously, who knows, but it was Whitman who became my comrade for what turned out to be, rather, an expedition. Into a text yet unknown to the three of us. These two poets couldn't be more different, and yet so many similarities began to come to the surface. Limbs, for instance, and the body of the lover. As if they needed to be read side by side. But how dissimilar the bodies were, too. The one almost liquid, melting away on the streets of a city of dust, defined by repeating another island, an ugly city over which the I has no control whatsoever. The other, an athletic body full of exclamation points, ready to traverse a vast landscape, all his own. Language has the habit of bringing things together that lie awkwardly next to each other, what if these two were lovers? A horrendous love it'd be. To bring together the poets of two nations is also to bring together the histories of these nations. These nations are already awkwardly close. A proximity so violent and unloving it'd be fatally tone-deaf to use love as a metaphor here. And yet I did it! But not to celebrate this union through a fantasy of mutual consent and eroticism. Whitman's foundational athletics are dismembered and melted down in the impossibility of the colonial situation. I asked the non-optimistic voice to take over, to enthusiastically renounce the hopes of tamable landscapes and sing the erasure of the tropes of foundational histories. Through desire, yes, I contradict myself. A desire of not!

Acknowledgments

I dreamed this book on board the M train in the New York City subway, at a time when I rode it daily from Ridgewood to Columbia University, keeping my thoughts in a *New York Review of Books* red notebook and listening to The Magnetic Fields' *69 Love Songs*; I found much inspiration while working my Saturday shifts at Topos Bookstore; I wrote "Sunday Expeditions" for a class with Paul Muldoon; by then it was another fall and I spent hours on Sundays sitting on a bench at Riverside Park, facing the Hudson River. I thank the city, the subway, Stephin Merritt, the bookstore, the university, the park, the river, the seasons, my incredibly small studio, and the intense loneliness of those years. They made me dream of multitudes. I finished the book in my apartment in Puerto Rico during the pandemic, in the company of my cats Corinna, Safo, and Lola, in the loving observation of their infinitely tender and amusing behavior.

I read earlier versions of parts of the book at different poetry events in New York and San Juan: The Mall of Found Artist Residency (New Lebanon, NY), Us & Them: A Writer-Translator Reading Series (Molasses Books, Brooklyn), Crush #6 (Woodbine, Ridgewood), Mount Lebanon Marathon Reading (New Lebanon, NY), Museo de Arte de Puerto Rico, and Este borde no es una frontera (San Juan, Puerto Rico). I want to thank the organizers of those events, because reading to an audience was essential to the book's development. At those readings, I received encouragement without which I would not have finished it from Sarah Steadman, Sam Bett and Tom Portnowitz, Susan Goldenberg, Xavier Valcárcel, Raquel Salas Rivera, and Irizelma Robles. Raquel, Irizelma, and Margarita Pintado read versions of the manuscript and I thank them for their comments and support. I am also grateful to Luis Othoniel Rosa for his enthusiastic reading.

The early seeds of this book are in a few poems that did not make it into the final manuscript, but I want to thank Ben Lerner for the generous feedback he gave me back then at Brooklyn College. A class with Ammiel Alcalay at Queens College was also essential for the meditations behind this book. Finally, I am forever indebted to my beloved friends Jacqui Cornetta and Kira Josefsson for the company throughout the years.

This is a revised edition of the book previously published in 2022 in Puerto Rico by La secta de los perros. I thank the editor and publisher, Rafael Acevedo, for his generous support of my work, and I also thank my friend Emanuel Torres for the drawing used on the cover of that first edition. In this revised second edition, I have added two poems in Spanish in the section "Canto primero."

Puerto Rican writer and translator **CRISTINA PÉREZ DÍAZ** holds a PhD in Classics from Columbia University and a Masters in Philosophy from the National Autonomous University of Mexico. Her critical bilingual edition of José Watanabe's *Antígona* was published by Routledge and won the 2023 ASTR Translation Prize. She has published two chapbooks of poetry in Spanish: *Adentro crían pájaros* (Parawa) and *Nueva anatomía imaginaria* (La impresora). Her poems and translations have appeared in *Asymptote, Words Without Borders, Hayden's Ferry, Eterna Cadencia,* and *Periódico de Poesía,* among other journals. She teaches Comparative Literature at the University of Puerto Rico (Río Piedras).

From the Founding of the Country
Copyright © Cristina Pérez Díaz, 2025

ISBN 978-1-959708-13-1
LCCN 2025930678

First Edition, 2025 — 1,000 copies

Winter Editions, Brooklyn, New York
wintereditions.net

The cover features a detail of a drawing by Suzanne Goldenberg: *ensemble* (2019).

WE books are typeset in Heldane, a renaissance-inspired serif designed by Kris Sowersby for Klim Type Foundry, and Zirkon, a contemporary gothic designed by Tobias Rechsteiner for Grilli Type. The layout and covers are done by the editor following a series design by Andrew Bourne.

This book was printed and bound in Lithuania by BALTO print with eco-friendly Munken papers. Manufactured by Arctic Paper in Sweden, Munken meets EU Ecolabel, Forest Stewardship Council, and Cradle to Cradle certification standards.

WE is grateful for the support of our subscribers, and extends special thanks to recent Supporting and Lifetime Subscribers: Anonymous, Anonymous (in memory of the Beaubiens), Yevgeniy Fiks, Elizabeth T. Gray, Jr., and Katy Lederer.

WE is a member of the Community of Literary Magazines and Presses (CLMP). Our 2025 program is supported by a Small Press Future Fund grant from CLMP and the Mellon Foundation.

Winter Editions

Emily Simon, IN MANY WAYS

Garth Graeper, THE SKY BROKE MORE

Robert Desnos, NIGHT OF LOVELESS NIGHTS, tr. Lewis Warsh

Richard Hell, WHAT JUST HAPPENED

Marina Temkina & Michel Gérard, BOYS FIGHT

Claire DeVoogd, VIA

Morica McClure, THE GONE THING

Ahmad Almallah, BORDER WISDOM

Hélio Oiticica, SECRET POETICS, tr. Rebecca Kosick

Heimrad Bäcker, DOCUMENTARY POETRY, tr. Patrick Greaney

Robert Fitterman, CREVE COEUR

Karla Kelsey, TRANSCENDENTAL FACTORY: FOR MINA LOY

Alan Gilbert, THE EVERYDAY LIFE OF DESIGN

Betsy Fagin, FIRES SEEN FROM SPACE

Cristina Pérez Díaz, FROM THE FOUNDING OF THE COUNTRY

Sarah Riggs, LINES

Leah Flax Barber, THE MIRROR OF SIMPLE SOULS

Michael Kasper, START ANYWHERE

POSTCARDS OF THE SIEGE: VISUAL CULTURE DURING THE SIEGE OF LENINGRAD (1941–1944), ed. Polina Barskova

Nathalie Quintane, THE CAVALIER, tr. Jonathan Larson

Monique Wittig, THE LESBIAN BODY, tr. David LeVay

Monique Wittig, ACROSS THE ACHERON, tr. David LeVay